Easy Learning

Oracle SQL

YANG HU

Simple is the beginning of wisdom. From the essence of practice, to briefly explain the concept, and vividly cultivate programming interest, this book deeply analyzes Oracle SQL programming, you will learn easy and well.

http://en.verejava.com

Copyright © 2019 Yang Hu

ISBN: 9781094789101

CONTENTS

1. Oracle Installation 3

2. Data Manipulation Language 5

3. Tablespace 6

4. User 8

5. Data Type 9

6. Insert Data 10

7. Update Data 18

8. Delete Data 20

9. Transaction 22

10. Constraints 24

11. One to One Association Table 28

12. One to Many Association Table 31

13. Many to Many Association Table 34

14. Constraint Management 37

15. Function 38

16. Group By 44

17. Inner Join 45

18. Outer Join 47

19. Seft Join 53

20. Sub Query 55

21. Multi Row SubQuery 57

22. Get Top N Rows 60

23. Paging Query 62

24. Collection 64

25. View 69

26. SEQUENCE 70

27. Procedure 73

28. PL/SQL 79

   28.1 IF Statement 79

   28.2 Case Statement 82

   28.3 While Loop 85

   28.4 For Loop 87

29. Cursor 89
   29.1 For Loop Cursor 91
   29.2 Fetch Cursor 92
30. Trigger 93

Oracle Installation

Click link to install Oracle:

http://en.verejava.com/?id=2534761766911

Open Command Console in Window

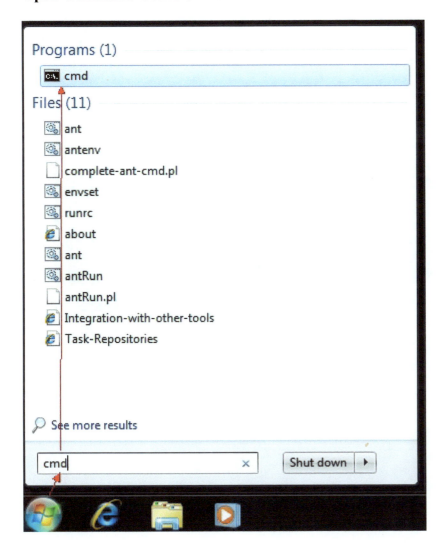

Login oracle by cmd username : scott password : you set before like: verejava1981

Sqlplus scott/verejava1981

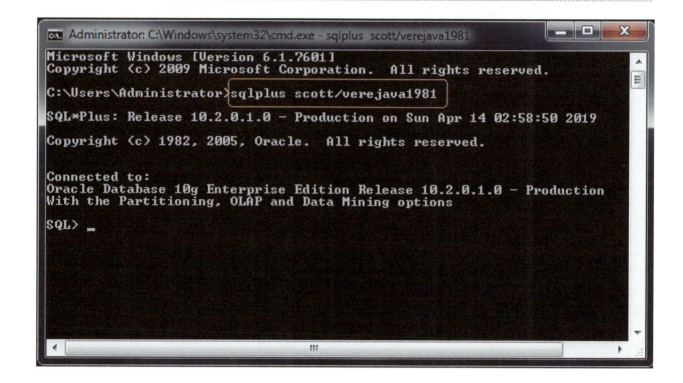

Data Manipulation Language

Login as dba, username : scott password : you set before like: verejava1981

sqlplus system/verejava1981 as sysdba

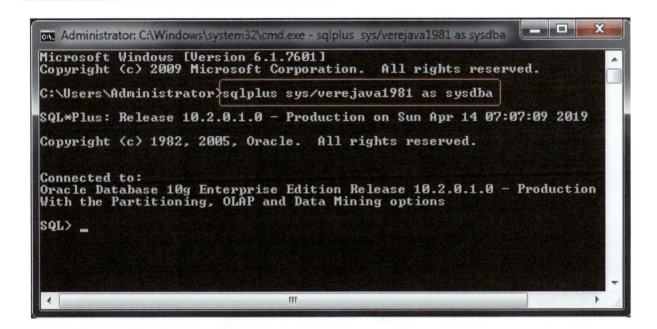

Shut down the database immediately

shutdown immediate

Startup the database

startup

Tablespace

Tablespace: Oracle divides a database into one or more logical storage units.

Each tablespace consists of one or more files called datafiles. A datafile physically stores the data objects of the database such as tables and indexes on disk.

View database table space

SELECT * FROM V$TABLESPACE;

Show where the database file is associated with table space

SELECT name FROM V$DATAFILE;

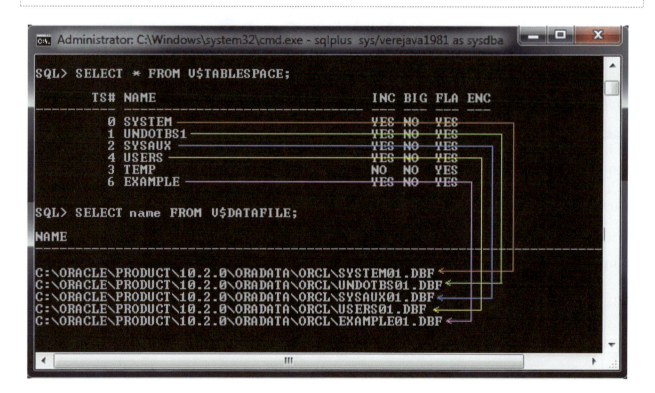

TEMP: is the temporary tablespace which is used for storing intermediate results of sorting, hashing, and large object processing operations. Temp file in DBA_TEMP_FILES.

Create a database tablespace: myspace

CREATE TABLESPACE myspace DATAFILE
'C:/ORACLE/PRODUCT/10.2.0/ORADATA/ORCL/myspace.dbf' SIZE 300m;

Delete tablespaces: myspace including content, data files, and constraints

DROP TABLESPACE myspace INCLUDING CONTENTS AND DATAFILES CASCADE
CONSTRAINTS;

User

User: is an account through which you can log in to the database

Create a User: myspace, Password: myspace123 in TableSpace: myspace

CREATE USER myspace IDENTIFIED BY myspace123 DEFAULT TABLESPACE myspace;

Modify user password to: myspace456

ALTER USER myspace IDENTIFIED BY myspace456;

When you create a user, the user's privilege domain is empty. To log on to Oracle Database, a user must have the system privilege. Therefore, after creating a user, you should grant the user privilege like: CREATE SESSION, RESOURCE, CONNECT, DBA etc.

Grant user: myspace privilege

GRANT DBA, RESOURCE, CONNECT TO   myspace;

Remove user: myspace privilege

REVOKE RESOURCE, CONNECT FROM   myspace;

Delete user: myspace and also drops all owned objects with CASCADE

DROP USER myspace CASCADE;

Data Type

Oracle common data types

VARCHAR2	Variable-length character string.
NVARCHAR2	Variable-length Unicode character string having maximum length size characters.
NUMBER	Number having precision p and scale s.
FLOAT	A FLOAT value is represented internally as NUMBER.
DATE	Valid date range : From January 1, 4712 BC, to December 31, 9999 AD.
TIMESTAMP	This data type contains the datetime fields YEAR, MONTH, DAY, HOUR, MINUTE, and SECOND.
CHAR	Fixed-length character data of length size bytes or characters.
CLOB	A character large object containing single-byte or multibyte characters.
BLOB	A binary large object.

Insert Data

INSERT INTO Table Name (Field Name **...**)**VALUES**(Field Value **...**);

Login username : scott password : you set before like: verejava1981

sqlplus scott/verejava1981

Delete table: emp

DROP TABLE emp;

Create a table: emp

CREATE TABLE emp
(
    id NUMBER(10),
    name VARCHAR2(20),
    salary NUMBER(10,2),
    birth DATE
);

```
Administrator: C:\Windows\system32\cmd.exe - sqlplus  sys/verejava1981 as sysdba

SQL> CREATE TABLE emp
  2  (
  3        id NUMBER(10),
  4        name VARCHAR2(20),
  5        salary NUMBER(10,2),
  6        birth DATE
  7  );

Table created.

SQL> desc emp;
 Name                                      Null?    Type
 -----------------------------------------------------------------------------

 ID                                                 NUMBER(10)
 NAME                                               VARCHAR2(20)
 SALARY                                             NUMBER(10,2)
 BIRTH                                              DATE

SQL>
```

1. Inserting records to all fields of table: emp

TO_DATE: converts CHAR, VARCHAR2 datatype to a value of DATE datatype.

```
INSERT INTO emp VALUES(1,'David',5000,TO_DATE('2002-11-22','yyyy-mm-dd'));
INSERT INTO emp VALUES(2,'James',6000,TO_DATE('2003-11-22','yyyy-mm-dd'));
INSERT INTO emp VALUES(3,'Grace',3000,TO_DATE('2000-11-22','yyyy-mm-dd'));
INSERT INTO emp VALUES(4,'Renia',7000,NULL);
```

```
Administrator: C:\Windows\system32\cmd.exe - sqlplus  sys/verejava1981 as sysdba

SQL> select * from emp;

    ID NAME                          SALARY BIRTH
                                    ---------- ---------
     1 David                          5000 22-NOV-02
     2 James                          6000 22-NOV-03
     3 Grace                          3000 22-NOV-00
     4 Renia                          7000
```

2. Insert records to some of the specified fields

```
INSERT INTO emp(id,name)VALUES(5,'Luka');
INSERT INTO emp(id,name,salary)VALUES(6,'Mathew',8000);
INSERT INTO emp(id,name,birth)VALUES(7,'Isacc',TO_DATE('2005-11-5','yyyy-mm-dd'));
```

```
Administrator: C:\Windows\system32\cmd.exe - sqlplus  sys/verejava1981 as sysdba

SQL> select * from emp;

    ID NAME                          SALARY BIRTH
                                    ---------- ---------
     1 David                          5000 22-NOV-02
     2 James                          6000 22-NOV-03
     3 Grace                          3000 22-NOV-00
     4 Renia                          7000
     5 Luka
     6 Mathew                         8000
     7 Isacc                               05-NOV-05
```

3. Create table: temp_emp, and then insert data from anther table: emp

```
CREATE TABLE temp_emp
(
    id NUMBER(10),
    name VARCHAR2(20),
    salary NUMBER(10,2),
    birth DATE
);
```

And then insert data from anther table: emp

```
INSERT INTO temp_emp ( select * from emp );
```

```
SQL> INSERT INTO temp_emp ( select * from emp );


SQL> select * from temp_emp;
        ID NAME                     SALARY BIRTH
                                    ------ ---------
         1 David                      5000 22-NOV-02
         2 James                      6000 22-NOV-03
         3 Grace                      3000 22-NOV-00
         4 Renia                      7000
         5 Luka
         6 Mathew                     8000
         7 Isacc                            05-NOV-05
```

4. Insert data to specified fields from table: emp

INSERT INTO temp_emp(name,salary) (select name,salary from emp);

5. Insert data to table: temp_emp from multi-table

First create anther table: account

```
CREATE TABLE account
(
    id NUMBER(10),
    name VARCHAR2(20),
    age NUMBER(3)
);
```

Insert data into table: account

```
INSERT INTO account VALUES(1,'Ablaham',30);
INSERT INTO account VALUES(2,'Sala',40);
INSERT INTO account VALUES(3,'John',20);
```

Insert data into the table: temp_emp from account union emp

```
INSERT INTO temp_emp(name,salary)
(
    SELECT name,0 FROM account
    UNION
    SELECT name,salary FROM emp
);
```

6. Insert data from table: emp into multiple tables: temp_emp, temp_emp2, temp_emp3

```
INSERT [ALL | FIRST]
WHEN <Condition> THEN INTO <Table>
WHEN < Condition > THEN INTO < Table >
......
[ELSE INTO <Other Table>]
```

ALL: If a record has been inserted into the previous <table>, it will continue to insert the following <table>

FIRST: If a record has been inserted into the previous <table>, it will not be inserted following <table>.

First Create anther 2 tables: temp_emp2, temp_emp3

```
CREATE TABLE temp_emp2
(
    id NUMBER(10),
    name VARCHAR2(20),
    salary NUMBER(10,2),
    birth DATE
);

CREATE TABLE temp_emp3
(
    id NUMBER(10),
    name VARCHAR2(20),
    salary NUMBER(10,2),
    birth DATE
);
```

And then delete data from 3 tables: temp_emp, temp_emp2, temp_emp3

```
DELETE FROM temp_emp;

DELETE FROM temp_emp2;

DELETE FROM temp_emp3;
```

Insert data from table: emp to tables: temp_emp, temp_emp2, temp_emp3

```
INSERT ALL
WHEN salary<=5000 THEN INTO temp_emp
WHEN salary=6000 THEN INTO temp_emp2
ELSE INTO temp_emp3
SELECT * FROM emp;
```

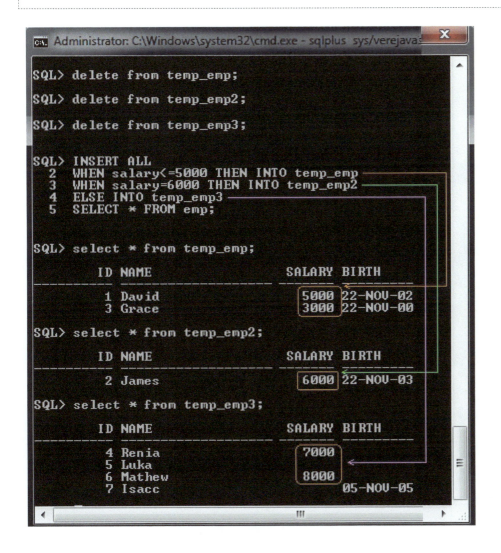

Update Data

UPDATE Table
SET Field=Value , .Field=Value , ...
[WHERE Condition]

1. Add $200 for everyone's salary from table: emp

UPDATE emp SET salary=salary+200;

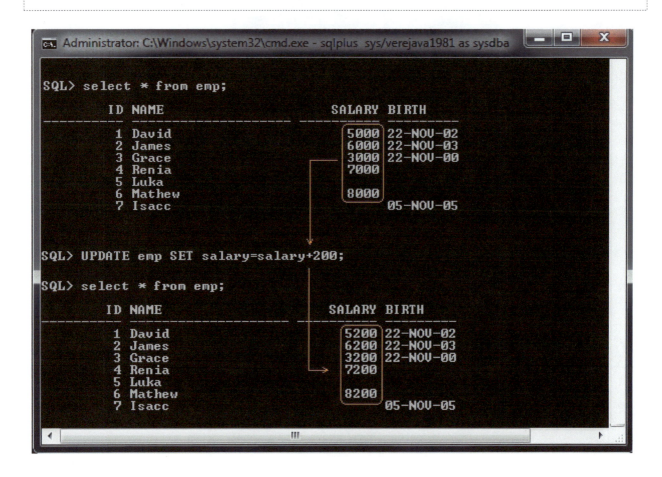

2. David's salary increment 500

UPDATE emp SET salary=salary+500 WHERE name='David';

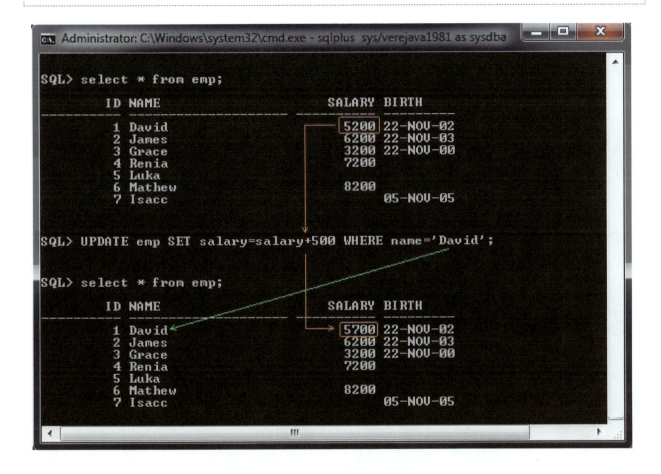

Delete Data

DELETE [FROM] Table **[WHERE** Condition]

1. Delete data from table: emp, the condition id = 1

DELETE FROM emp WHERE id=1;

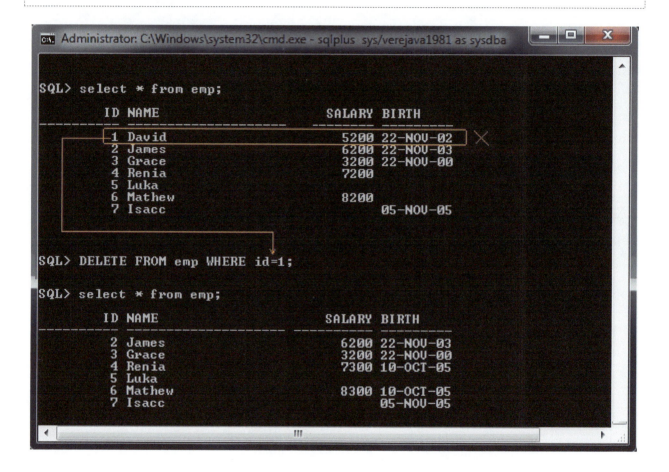

2. Delete data from table: emp, the condition is salary between 3000 and 7000

DELETE FROM emp WHERE salary>3000 AND salary<7000;

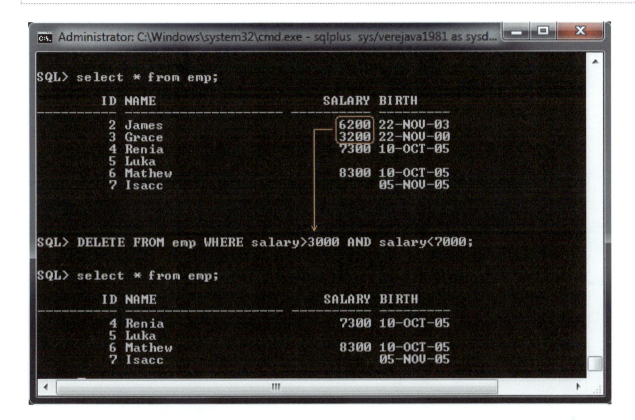

3. Delete all data from table: emp

DELETE FROM emp;

Transaction

Transaction: is a logical, atomic unit of work that contains one or more SQL statements that all succeed **COMMIT** or all fail **ROLLBACK**.

1. Insert a piece of data to table: emp, and then COMMIT

INSERT INTO emp VALUES(1,'David',8000,TO_DATE('2007-7-7','yyyy-mm-dd'));
INSERT INTO emp VALUES(2,'Grace',6000,TO_DATE('2008-8-8','yyyy-mm-dd'));
COMMIT;

```
SQL> select * from emp;

        ID NAME                          SALARY BIRTH
---------- -------------------- --------------- ---------
         1 David                           8000 07-JUL-07
         2 Grace                           6000 08-AUG-08
```

2. Insert a piece of data to table: emp, and then ROLLBACK

INSERT INTO emp VALUES(3,'Rache',5000,TO_DATE('2009-9-9','yyyy-mm-dd'));
ROLLBACK;

```
SQL> INSERT INTO emp VALUES(3,'Rache',5000,TO_DATE('2009-9-9','yyyy-

SQL> select * from emp;

        ID NAME                          SALARY BIRTH
---------- -------------------- --------------- ---------
         1 David                           8000 07-JUL-07
         2 Grace                           6000 08-AUG-08
         3 Rache                           5000 09-SEP-09

SQL> ROLLBACK;

SQL> select * from emp;

        ID NAME                          SALARY BIRTH
---------- -------------------- --------------- ---------
         1 David                           8000 07-JUL-07
         2 Grace                           6000 08-AUG-08
```

2. SAVEPOINT: Use the SAVEPOINT statement to identify a point in a transaction to which you can later roll back.

```
UPDATE emp SET salary=9000 WHERE name='David';
SAVEPOINT p1;
DELETE FROM emp WHERE name='Grace';
SELECT * FROM emp;
ROLLBACK TO p1;
SELECT * FROM emp;
```

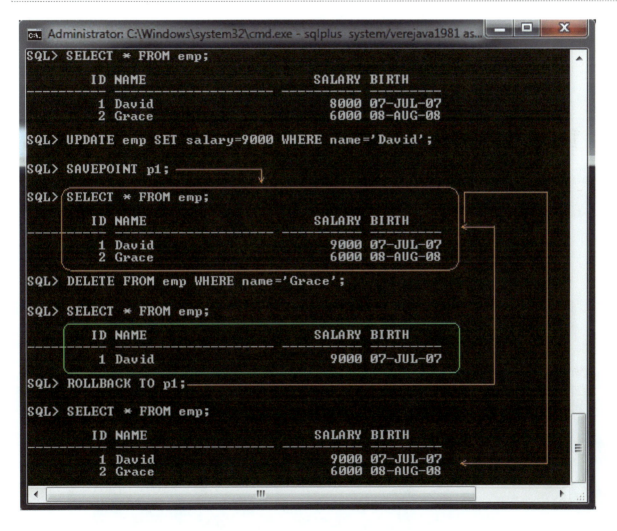

Constraints

Oracle database constraints include:
NOT NULL
UNIQUE
CHECK
PRIMARY KEY
FOREIGN KEY

1. NOT NULL

If a field has a **NOT NULL** constraint, the field must be given a value

```
CREATE TABLE student
(
    id NUMBER(10) NOT NULL,
    name VARCHAR2(30) NOT NULL
);
```

Insert values to check the legality

```
INSERT INTO student VALUES(1,'David');
INSERT INTO student VALUES(2,NULL);
INSERT INTO student(name)VALUES('Grace');
```

2. Check

A check constraint allows you to specify a condition on each row in a table.

```sql
CREATE TABLE account
(
    username VARCHAR2(50) PRIMARY KEY,
    pwd VARCHAR2(50),
    age NUMBER(3) ,
    CHECK(age>=0 AND age<=130),
    CHECK(length(trim(username))>=6)
);
```

Insert values to check the legality

```sql
INSERT INTO account(username,pwd,age)VALUES('Andrew','111',40);
INSERT INTO account(username,pwd,age)VALUES('Andrew','111',-1);
INSERT INTO account(username,pwd,age)VALUES(David,'111',160);
```

3. UNIQUE
This field cannot have duplicate values

```
DROP TABLE student;

CREATE TABLE student
(
    id NUMBER(10),
    name VARCHAR2(30) NOT NULL,
    CONSTRAINT student_id_unique UNIQUE(id)
);
```

Insert values to check the legality

```
INSERT INTO student VALUES(1,'David');
INSERT INTO student VALUES(2,'David');
INSERT INTO student VALUES(1,'David');
```

4. PRIMARY KEY
This field cannot have duplicate values and not null

```
DROP TABLE student;

CREATE TABLE student
(
    id NUMBER(10),
    name VARCHAR2(30) NOT NULL,
    CONSTRAINT student_id_unique PRIMARY KEY(id)
);
```

Insert values to check the legality

```
INSERT INTO student VALUES(1,'David');
INSERT INTO student VALUES(1,'David');
INSERT INTO student VALUES(NULL,'David');
```

One to One Association Table

FOREIGN KEY

1. The foreign key must refer to the primary key or unique key of the primary table.
2. When the primary key or unique key of the primary table is referenced by the child table, the record corresponding to the primary table is not allowed to be deleted.

```sql
DROP TABLE emp;

CREATE TABLE emp
(

  id NUMBER(10) PRIMARY KEY,
  name VARCHAR2(30),
  job VARCHAR2(30)
);

CREATE TABLE salary
(

  id NUMBER(10) PRIMARY KEY,
  emp_id NUMBER(10),
  salary NUMBER(8,2),
  CONSTRAINT salary_id_fk FOREIGN KEY(emp_id) REFERENCES emp(id)
);
```

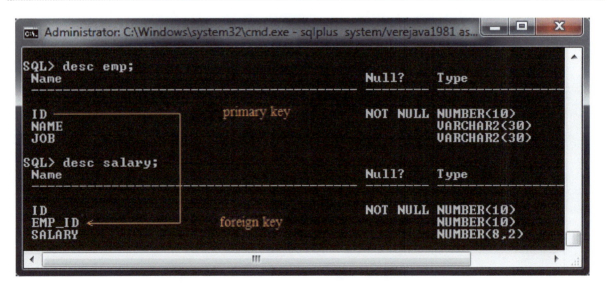

28

Insert data into table: emp

INSERT INTO emp(id,name,job)VALUES(1,'David','Programmer');
INSERT INTO emp(id,name,job)VALUES(2,'Grace','Testing');

Insert data into table: salary

INSERT INTO salary(id,emp_id,salary)VALUES(1,1,5000);
INSERT INTO salary(id,emp_id,salary)VALUES(2,2,6000);

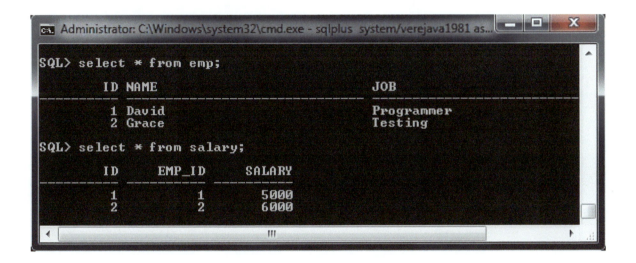

Query all emp.name and his salary.
Alias: emp as a, salary as b

SELECT a.name ,b.salary FROM emp a,salary b WHERE a.id=b.emp_id ;

```
SQL> select * from emp;

        ID NAME                              JOB
---------- --------------------------------- ----------------------
         1 David                             Programmer
         2 Grace                             Testing

SQL> select * from salary;

        ID     EMP_ID        SALARY
---------- ---------- ------------
         1          1         5000
         2          2         6000

SQL> SELECT a.name ,b.salary  FROM emp a,salary b WHERE a.id=b.emp_id ;

NAME                              SALARY
--------------------------------- ----------
David                               5000
Grace                               6000
```

30

One to Many Association Table

```sql
DROP TABLE dept;

CREATE TABLE dept
(
    id NUMBER(10) PRIMARY KEY,
    name VARCHAR2(10)
);

DROP TABLE salary;
DROP TABLE emp;

CREATE TABLE emp
(
    id NUMBER(10),
    name VARCHAR2(10),
    salary NUMBER(10),
    dept_id NUMBER(10) REFERENCES dept(id)
);
```

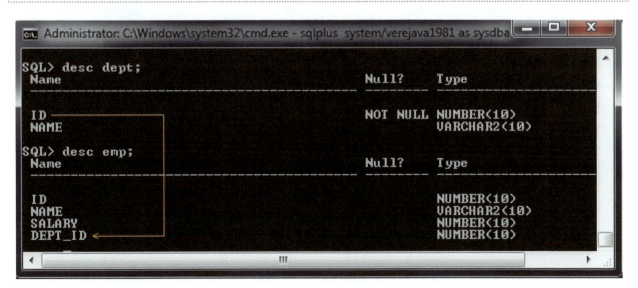

Insert data into table: dept

```
INSERT INTO dept(id,name)VALUES(1,'IT');
INSERT INTO dept(id,name)VALUES(2,'Finance');
```

Insert data into table: emp

```
INSERT INTO emp(id,name,salary,dept_id)VALUES(1,'David',6000,1);
INSERT INTO emp(id,name,salary,dept_id)VALUES(2,'James',5000,1);
INSERT INTO emp(id,name,salary,dept_id)VALUES(3,'Grace',6000,2);
INSERT INTO emp(id,name,salary,dept_id)VALUES(4,'Isacc',8000,2);
```

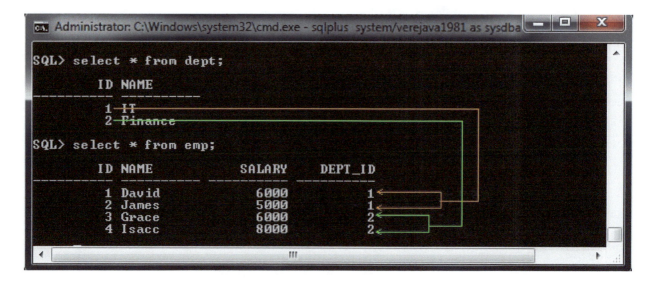

Query all emp.* and dept.name from tables: emp and dept

SELECT b.*,a.name FROM dept a,emp b WHERE a.id=b.dept_id ;

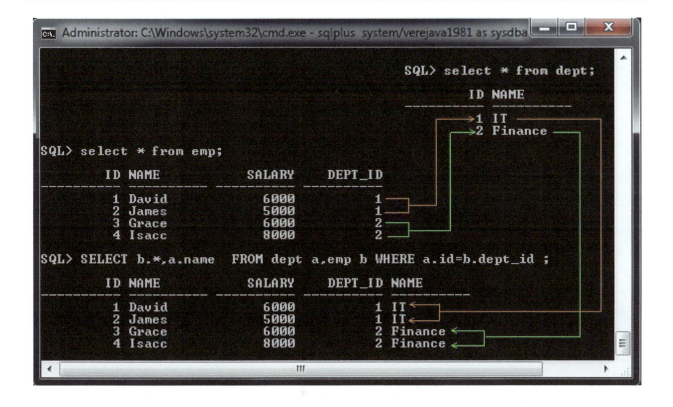

Many to Many Association Table

```sql
DROP TABLE teacher;
DROP TABLE student;

CREATE TABLE teacher
(
  id NUMBER(10) PRIMARY KEY,
  name VARCHAR2(20)
);

CREATE TABLE student
(
  id NUMBER(10) PRIMARY KEY,
  name VARCHAR2(20)
);

CREATE TABLE teacher_student
(
  teacher_id NUMBER(10),
  student_id NUMBER(10),
  CONSTRAINT teacher_id_fk FOREIGN KEY(teacher_id) REFERENCES teacher(id),
  CONSTRAINT student_id_fk FOREIGN KEY(student_id) REFERENCES student(id)
);
```

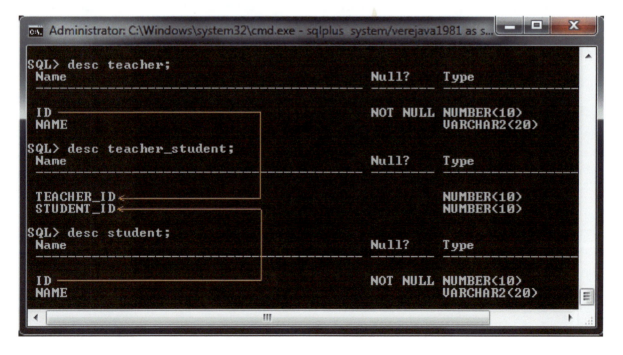

Insert data into table: teacher

INSERT INTO teacher(id,name)VALUES(1,'Teacher David');
INSERT INTO teacher(id,name)VALUES(2,'Teacher James');
INSERT INTO teacher(id,name)VALUES(3,'Teacher Isacc');

Insert data into table: student

INSERT INTO student(id,name)VALUES(1,'Grace');
INSERT INTO student(id,name)VALUES(2,'Renia');
INSERT INTO student(id,name)VALUES(3,'Gaja');
INSERT INTO student(id,name)VALUES(4,'Lida');

Insert data into table: teacher_student

INSERT INTO teacher_student(teacher_id,student_id)VALUES(1,1);
INSERT INTO teacher_student(teacher_id,student_id)VALUES(1,2);
INSERT INTO teacher_student(teacher_id,student_id)VALUES(2,2);
INSERT INTO teacher_student(teacher_id,student_id)VALUES(2,3);
INSERT INTO teacher_student(teacher_id,student_id)VALUES(2,4);

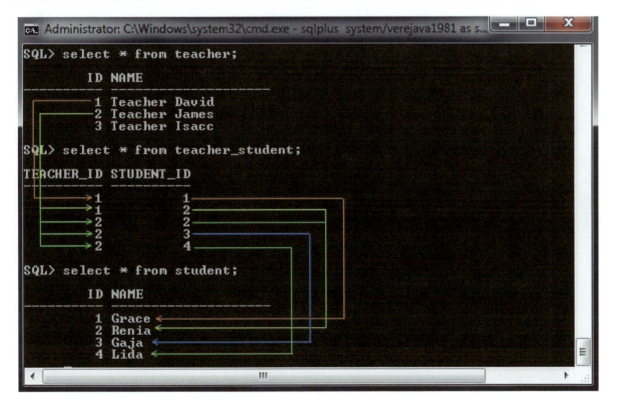

Find all data from tables: student ,teacher.

SELECT a.name teacher,c.name student
FROM teacher a, teacher_student b,student c
WHERE a.id=b.teacher_id AND b.student_id=c.id;

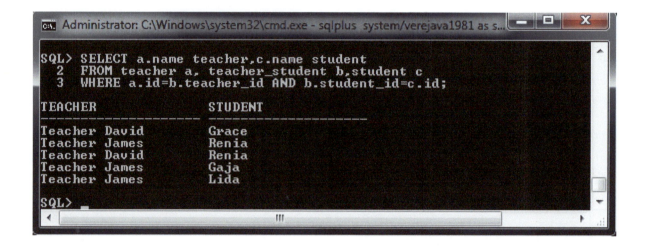

Constraint Management

1. View Constraint

```
SELECT owner,constraint_name,constraint_type FROM user_constraints;
```

P : Primary Key
R : Foreign Key
U : Unique
C : Not Null or Check

2. Add Constraint

```
DROP TABLE student;

CREATE TABLE student
(
   id NUMBER(10),
   name VARCHAR2(50)
);

INSERT INTO student VALUES(1,'David');
INSERT INTO student VALUES(1,'David');
```

3. Add Constaint

```
ALTER TABLE student ADD CONSTRAINT student_id_pk PRIMARY KEY(id);
```

4. Delete Constraint

```
ALTER TABLE Table DROP CONSTRAINT constraint_name [CASCADE]
```

Function

1. Char Function

lower():converts all letters in the specified string to lowercase

```
SELECT lower('JOSEPH') FROM dual;
joseph
```

upper():converts all letters in the specified string to uppercase

```
SELECT upper('Joseph') FROM dual;
JOSEPH
```

initcap(): sets the first character in each word to uppercase and the rest to lowercase

```
SELECT initcap('sally') FROM dual;
Sally
```

concat(): allows you to concatenate two strings together.

```
SELECT concat('Mr ','James') FROM dual;
Mr James
```

substr(): allows you to extract a substring from a string.

```
SELECT substr('test.txt',5,4) FROM dual;
.txt
```

length(): returns the length of the specified string.

```
SELECT length('Mr James') FROM dual;
8
```

instr(): returns the location of a substring in a string.

```
SELECT instr('Mr James','James') FROM dual;
4
```

lpad(): pads the left-side of a string with a specific set of characters

```
SELECT lpad('james',10,'*') FROM dual;
*****james
```

rpad(): pads the right-side of a string with a specific set of characters

```
SELECT rpad('james',10,'*') FROM dual;
james*****
```

trim(): removes all specified characters either from the beginning or the end of a string.

```
SELECT length(trim(' james '))  FROM dual;
james
```

replace(): replaces a sequence of characters in a string with another set of characters.

```
SELECT replace('Mr James','Mr','Mrs')  FROM dual;
Mrs James
```

2. Numeric Function

abs(): returns the absolute value of a number.

```
SELECT abs(-1)  FROM dual;
1
```

round(): returns a number rounded to a certain number of decimal places.

```
SELECT round(3.6)  FROM dual;
4
```

trunc(): returns a date truncated to a specific unit of measure.

```
SELECT trunc(3.14156,2)  FROM dual;
3.14
```

ceil(): returns the smallest integer value that is greater than or equal to a number.

```
SELECT ceil(3.14156)  FROM dual;
4
```

floor(): returns the largest integer value that is equal to or less than a number.

```
SELECT floor(3.14156)  FROM dual;
3
```

power(): returns m raised to the nth power.

```
SELECT power(4,2)  FROM dual;
16
```

sqrt(): returns the square root of n.

```
SELECT sqrt(9)  FROM dual;
3
```

mod(): returns the remainder of m divided by n.

```
SELECT mod(10,3)  FROM dual;
1
```

3. Date Function

```
SELECT to_char(sysdate,'yyyy-mm-dd hh24:mi:ss') as nowTime FROM dual;

SELECT to_char(sysdate,'yyyy')  as nowYear  FROM dual;

SELECT to_char(sysdate,'mm')    as nowMonth FROM dual;

SELECT to_char(sysdate,'dd')    as nowDay   FROM dual;

SELECT to_char(sysdate,'hh24')  as nowHour  FROM dual;

SELECT to_char(sysdate,'mi')    as nowMinute   FROM dual;

SELECT to_char(sysdate,'ss')    as nowSecond   FROM dual;

SELECT to_date('2004-05-07 13:23:44','yyyy-mm-dd hh24:mi:ss')   FROM dual;
```

4. Group Function

count(): returns the count of an expression.

SELECT count(*) FROM emp;

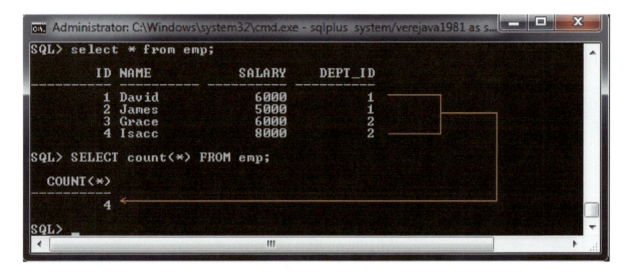

sum(): returns the summed value of an expression.

SELECT sum(salary) FROM emp;

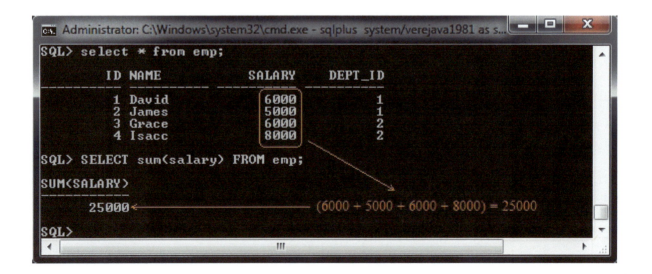

avg(): returns the average value of an expression.

SELECT avg(salary) FROM emp;

max(): returns the maximum value of an expression.

SELECT max(salary) FROM emp;

min(): returns the minimum value of an expression.

SELECT min(salary) FROM emp;

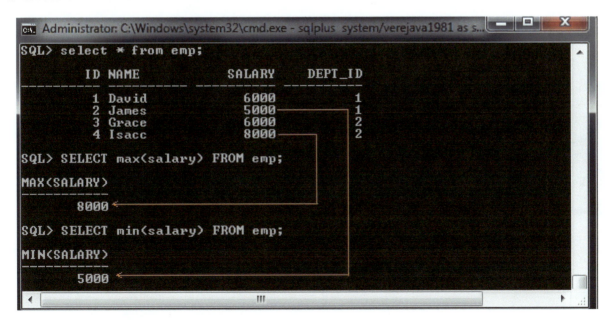

Group By

Calculate the average salary for each dept group

SELECT dept_id,avg(salary) FROM emp GROUP BY dept_id;

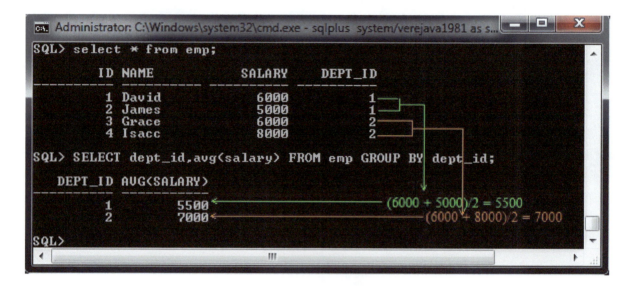

GROUP BY frist and then **HAVING**: like **WHERE**

SELECT dept_id,avg(salary) FROM emp GROUP BY dept_id
HAVING avg(salary)>6000;

Inner Join

Create 2 tables: emp, dept

```
DROP TABLE emp;
DROP TABLE dept;

CREATE TABLE dept
(
    id NUMBER(10) PRIMARY KEY,
    name VARCHAR2(10)
);

CREATE TABLE emp
(
    id NUMBER(10),
    name VARCHAR2(10),
    salary NUMBER(10),
    dept_id NUMBER(10) REFERENCES dept(id)
);
```

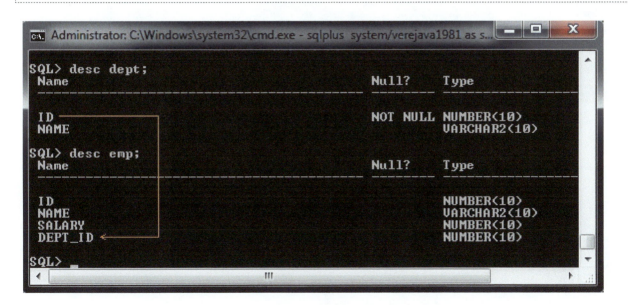

Insert data into table: dept

```
INSERT INTO dept(id,name)VALUES(1,'IT');
INSERT INTO dept(id,name)VALUES(2,'Finance');
```

Insert data into table: emp

```
INSERT INTO emp(id,name,salary,dept_id)VALUES(1,'David',6000,1);
INSERT INTO emp(id,name,salary,dept_id)VALUES(2,'Grace',5000,1);
INSERT INTO emp(id,name,salary,dept_id)VALUES(3,'James',6000,2);
INSERT INTO emp(id,name,salary,dept_id)VALUES(4,'Luka',8000,2);
```

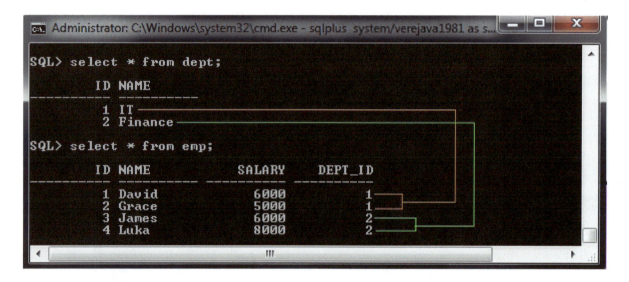

Display all data from tables: emp, dept with JOIN

```
SELECT b.*, a.name FROM dept a JOIN emp b  ON a.id=b.dept_id;
```

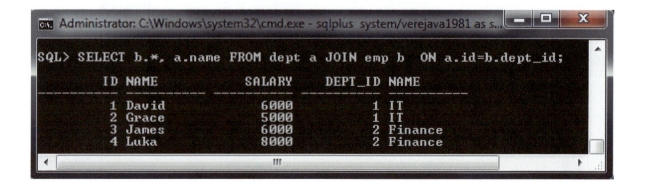

Outer Join

Create a table: car

```
CREATE TABLE car
(
    id NUMBER(10),
    producer VARCHAR2(15),
    model VARCHAR2(10),
    price NUMBER(10,2)
);
```

Insert data into table: car

```
INSERT INTO car(id,producer,model,price)VALUES(1,' Shanghai',' Santana',150000);
INSERT INTO car(id,producer,model,price)VALUES(2,' German',' Audi',400000);
INSERT INTO car(id,producer,model,price)VALUES(3,' FAW Volkswagen',' Audi A6',500000);
INSERT INTO car(id,producer,model,price)VALUES(4,' Beijing Benz',' Benz 280',1000000);
```

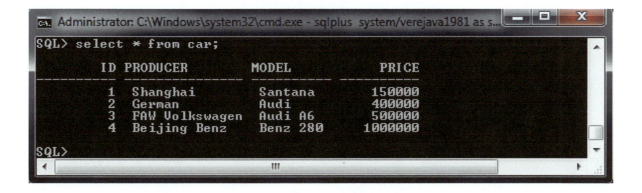

Add a column car_id into the table: emp

ALTER TABLE emp add(car_id NUMBER(10));

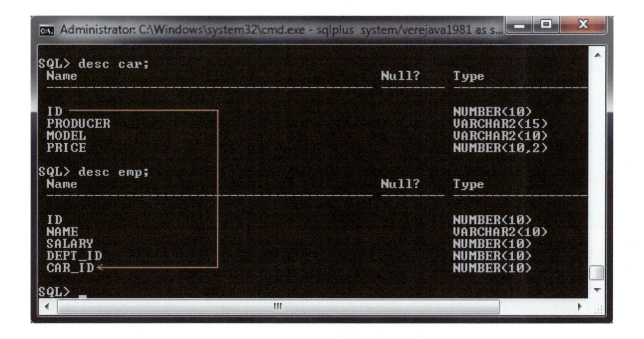

Set David own Shanghai car_id=1, Grace owns German car_id=2

UPDATE emp SET car_id=1 WHERE name='David';
UPDATE emp SET car_id=2 WHERE name='Grace';

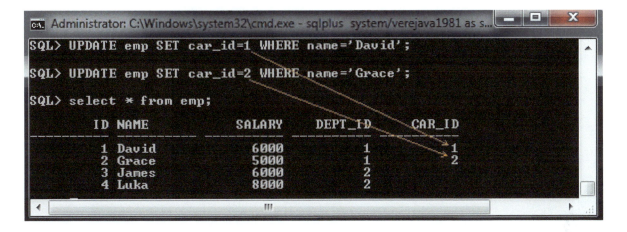

Find the emp's name and the emp's car

SELECT a.name, b.* FROM emp a,car b WHERE a.car_id=b.id;

LEFT JOIN: The left table does not match the data, the right table is filled with NULL

SELECT a.name, b.* FROM emp a LEFT JOIN car b ON a.car_id=b.id;

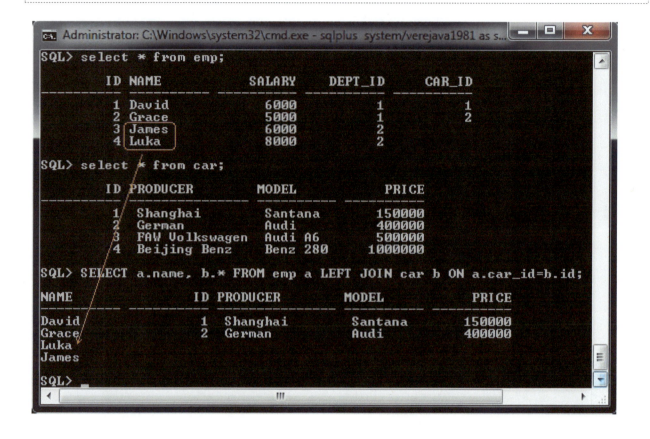

RIGHT JOIN: The rihgt table does not match the data, the left table is filled with NULL

SELECT a.name, b.* FROM emp a RIGHT JOIN car b ON a.car_id=b.id;

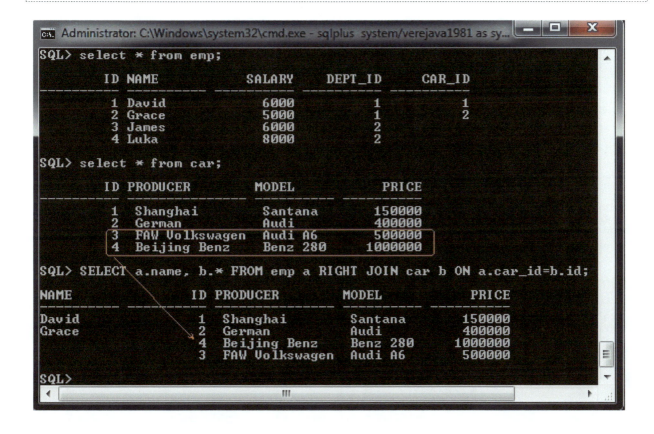

FULL JOIN: The left and right side table does not match the data fill with NULL

SELECT a.name, b.* FROM emp a FULL JOIN car b ON a.car_id=b.id;

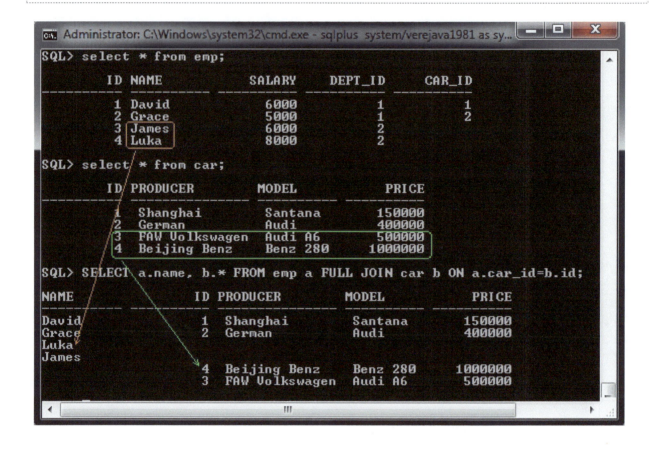

Seft Join

Create a table: category

```
CREATE TABLE category
(
   id NUMBER(10),
   name VARCHAR2(15),
   pid NUMBER(10)
);
```

Insert parent data into table: category

INSERT INTO category(id,name,pid)VALUES(1,'IT',0);
INSERT INTO category(id,name,pid)VALUES(2,'Book',0);

Insert child data into table: category

INSERT INTO category(id,name,pid)VALUES(100,' desktop',1);
INSERT INTO category(id,name,pid)VALUES(101,' notebook',1);
INSERT INTO category(id,name,pid)VALUES(200,' Anime Books',2);
INSERT INTO category(id,name,pid)VALUES(201,' fiction',2);

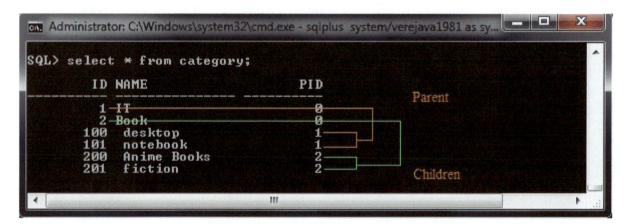

Query parent category and children category

SELECT a.name,b.name FROM category a JOIN category b ON a.pid=b.id;

Sub Query

Query all data of emp whose salary is greater than Grace's salary

SELECT * FROM emp
WHERE salary > (SELECT salary FROM emp WHERE name='Grace');

1. Analysis

First run
SELECT salary FROM emp WHERE name='Grace';   the result = 5000
And then run
SELECT * FROM emp WHERE salary > 5000;

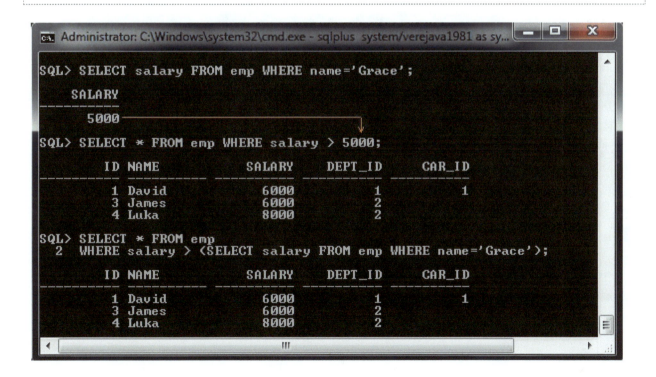

Find the dept_id whose average salary is higher than the average salary of emp.

SELECT dept_id,avg(salary) FROM emp GROUP BY dept_id HAVING avg(salary)>(SELECT avg(salary) FROM emp);

1. Analysis

First run
SELECT avg(salary) FROM emp;   the result = 6250
And then run
SELECT dept_id,avg(salary) FROM emp GROUP BY dept_id
HAVING avg(salary)>6250;

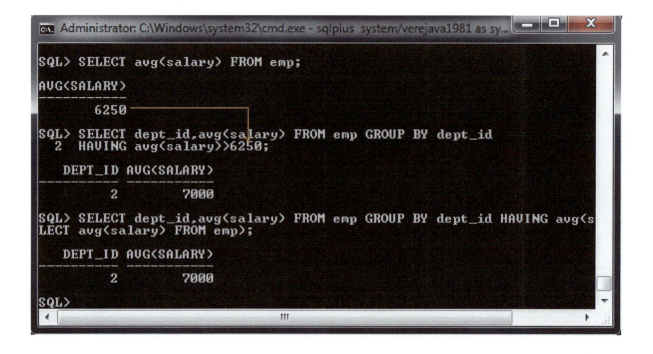

Multi Row SubQuery

IN: allows you to specify multiple values in a WHERE clause. id **IN** (3,4)
EXISTS: is used to test for the existence of any record in a subquery.**false or true**

Insert data into table: emp

INSERT INTO emp(id,name,salary,dept_id,car_id)VALUES(5,'Mathew',4000,1,3);
INSERT INTO emp(id,name,salary,dept_id,car_id)VALUES(6,'Luka',5000,1,3);
INSERT INTO emp(id,name,salary,dept_id,car_id)VALUES(7,'Lebeka',6000,2,3);
INSERT INTO emp(id,name,salary,dept_id,car_id)VALUES(8,'Make',8000,2,null);

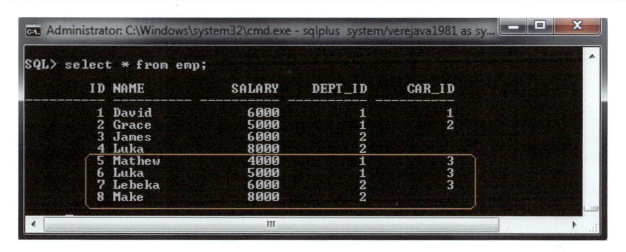

IN Find all employees that the dept_id the same as David or James

SELECT * FROM emp WHERE dept_id IN (SELECT dept_id FROM emp WHERE name='David' OR name='James');

1. Analysis

First run
SELECT dept_id FROM emp WHERE name='David' OR name='James';   the result = 1,2
And then run
SELECT * FROM emp WHERE dept_id IN(1,2);

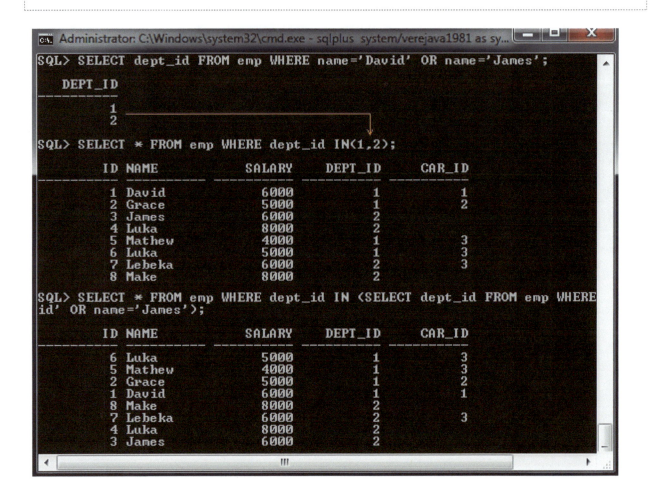

EXISTS If David's department exists, return all employees.

SELECT * FROM emp WHERE exists
(SELECT dept_id FROM emp WHERE name='David');

1. Analysis

First run
SELECT dept_id FROM emp WHERE name='David';   the result = true
Because the result = true **So run**
SELECT * FROM emp;

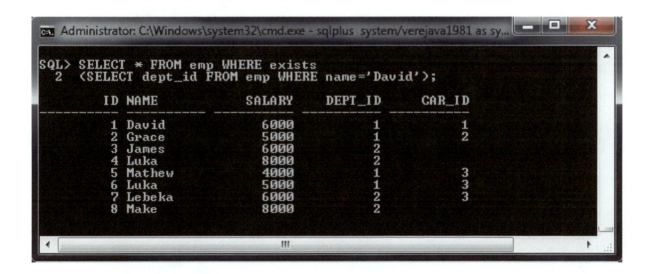

Get Top N Rows

1. Non-sorted query

ROWNUM: returns a number that represents the order that a row is selected by Oracle from a table or joined tables. The first row has a ROWNUM of 1… and so on.

Return the top 5 data from table: emp

SELECT ROWNUM ,emp.* FROM emp WHERE ROWNUM<=5;

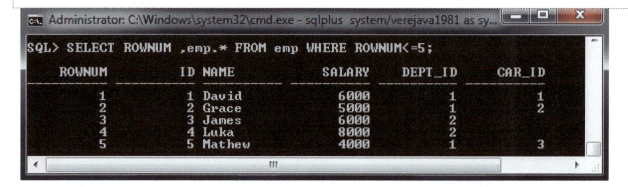

2. sorted query

Return the top 5 data from table: emp

SELECT ROWNUM ,emp.* FROM emp WHERE ROWNUM<=5 ORDER BY salary DESC;

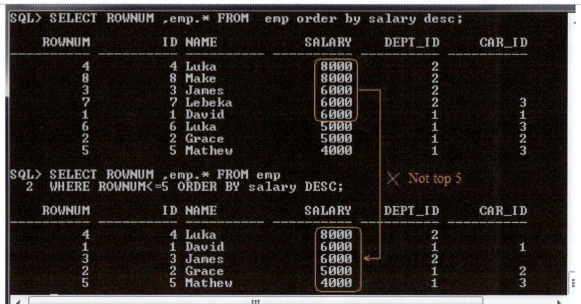

Result not top 5, because WHERE ROWNUM<=5 execute first and then ORDER BY salary DESC

If We want to get top 5, must ORDER BY salary DESC execute first and then
WHERE ROWNUM<=5

SELECT ROWNUM ,emp.* FROM
(SELECT * FROM emp ORDER BY salary DESC) emp
WHERE ROWNUM<=5;

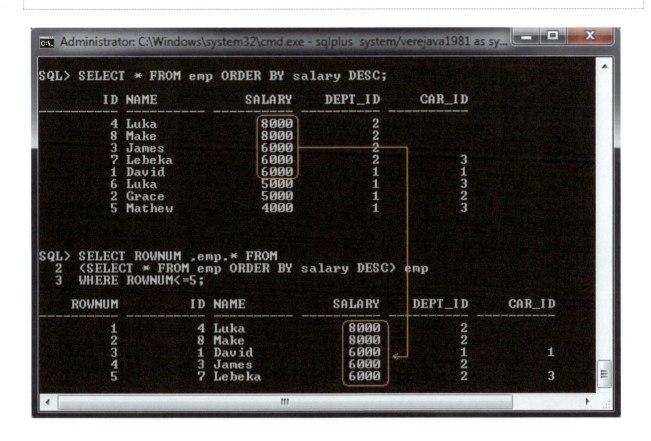

Paging Query

Sort by salary get 3 records per page, the first page

SELECT * FROM
(SELECT ROWNUM rn,emp.* FROM
(SELECT * FROM emp ORDER BY salary DESC) emp)
WHERE rn>3*(1-1) AND rn <=3*1;

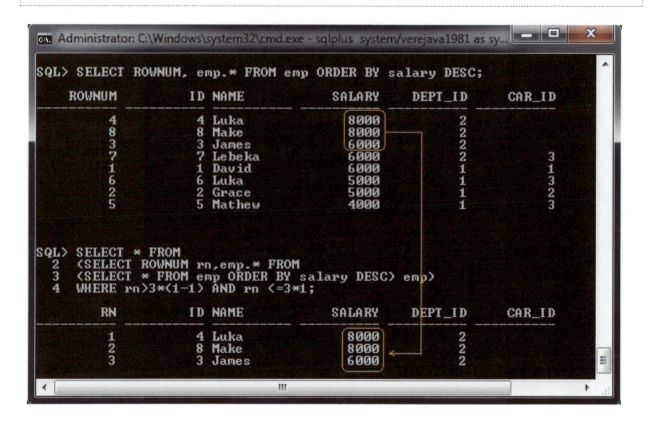

Sort by salary get 3 records per page, the secord page

SELECT * FROM
(SELECT ROWNUM rn,emp.* FROM
(SELECT * FROM emp ORDER BY salary DESC) emp)
WHERE rn>3*(2-1) AND rn <=3*2;

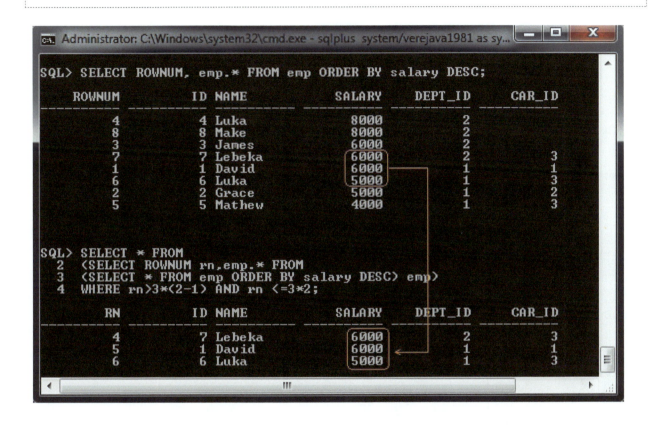

Collection

Collection:
UNION, INTERSECT, MINUS.

UNION: is used to combine the result sets of 2 or more Oracle SELECT statements.
(1,2,3) **UNION** (3,4,5) = (1,2,3,4,5)

INTERSECT: is used to return the results of 2 or more SELECT statements. If a record exists in one query and not in the other, it will be omitted from the INTERSECT results.
(1,2,3) **INTERSECT** (3,4,5) = (3)

MINUS: retrieve all records from the first dataset and then remove from the results all records from the second dataset.
(1,2,3) **MINUS** (3,4,5) = (1,2)

```sql
DROP TABLE account;

CREATE TABLE account
(
    id NUMBER(10),
    username VARCHAR2(10),
    pass VARCHAR2(10),
    name VARCHAR2(10)
);

INSERT INTO account(id,username, pass,name)VALUES(1,'Admin','111', 'Admin');
INSERT INTO account(id,username, pass,name)VALUES(2,'David','111', 'David');
INSERT INTO account(id,username, pass,name)VALUES(3,'Grace','111', 'Grace');
INSERT INTO account(id,username, pass,name)VALUES(4,'James','111', 'James');
```

UNION

Find all names from table: emp and account

```
SELECT name FROM emp
UNION
SELECT name FROM account;
```

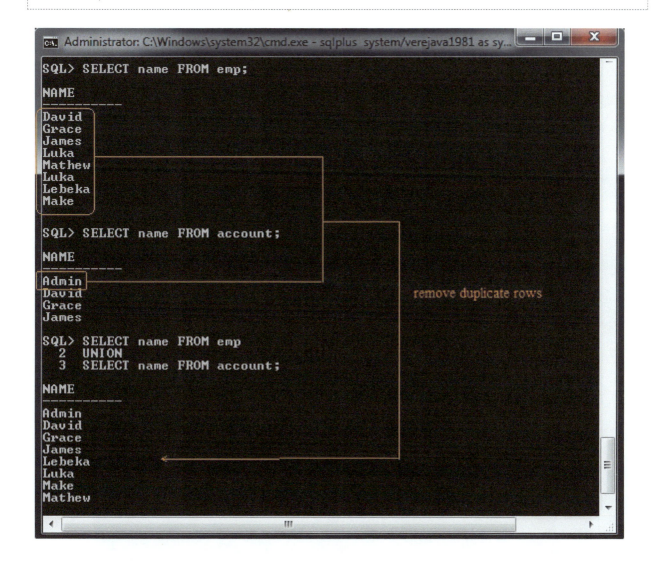

UNION ALL
Find all names from table: emp and account

SELECT name FROM emp
UNION ALL
SELECT name FROM account;

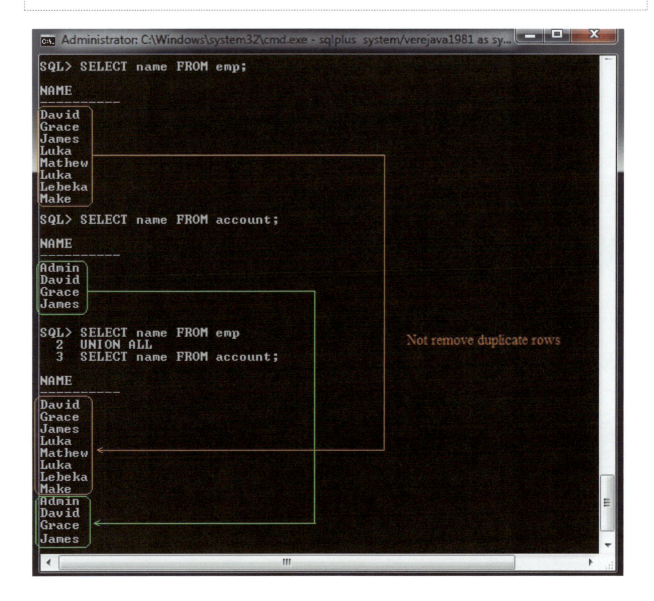

INTERSECT

SELECT name FROM emp
INTERSECT
SELECT name FROM account;

MINUS

SELECT name FROM emp
MINUS
SELECT name FROM account;

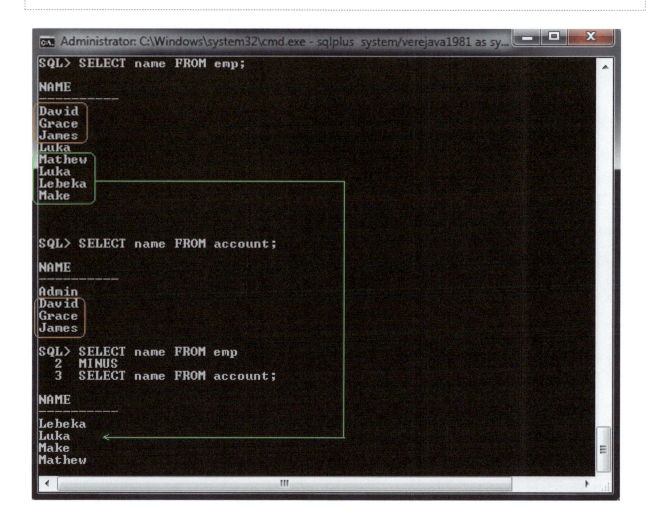

View

View: is a virtual table by extracting data from an actual table.

Create a view: dept_emp_view **showing the** max**,** min**,** average**, and** total **value of all employees salary in each department group**

CREATE VIEW dept_emp_view
AS SELECT d.name,max(e.salary) max,min(e.salary) min,avg(e.salary) avg,sum(e.salary) sum FROM dept d,emp e
WHERE d.id=e.dept_id GROUP BY d.name;

Display data from view: dept_emp_view

SELECT * FROM dept_emp_view;

Delete View: dept_emp_view

DROP VIEW dept_emp_view;

SEQUENCE

SEQUENCE: is an object in Oracle that is used to generate a number sequence. This can be useful when you need to create a unique number to act as a primary key.

1 .Create a sequence: emp_sequence

CREATE SEQUENCE emp_sequence INCREMENT BY 1 START WITH 1
NOMAXVALUE NOCYCLE;

2. Use sequence
1. **nextval**   The next value of the sequence
2. **currval**   Current value of the sequence

SELECT emp_sequence.nextval FROM dual;

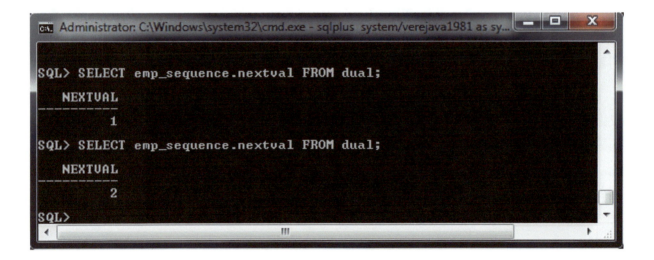

3. Insert the value of the id using the sequence

INSERT INTO emp(id,name,salary,dept_id)values(emp_sequence.nextval,'Sala',4000,2);

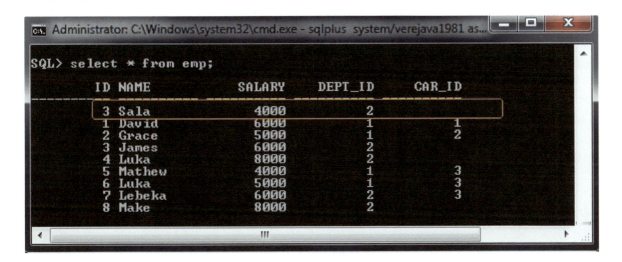

4. Delete sequence

DROP SEQUENCE emp_sequence

Index

Index: An index is a performance-tuning method of allowing faster retrieval of records.

Create a normal index based on the name

CREATE INDEX name_index ON emp(name);

Create a unique index based on id

CREATE UNIQUE INDEX id_unique_index ON emp(id);

View all indexes created by the table: emp

SELECT index_name,index_type FROM user_indexes WHERE table_name='EMP';

Delete indexes by index name

DROP INDEX index name

Procedure

Procedure: is a group of PL/SQL statements that you can call by name.

OUT Returned Value
IN   Parameter

```
CREATE OR REPLACE PROCEDURE name(param1 IN type,param2 OUT type）
AS
   Variable 1 type (value range);
   Variable 2 type (value range);
BEGIN

  DBMS_OUTPUT.put_line('information');

  EXCEPTION
    WHEN NO_DATA_FOUND THEN

  END;

END;
```

DBMS_OUTPUT.put_line execute: output message to console.

```
SET serveroutput ON;
```

Create a procedure: sp_get_dept_name **Get the dept name based on the dept id**

%TYPE: lets you declare a constant, variable, field, or parameter to be of the same data type a previously declared variable, field, record, nested table, or database column. If the referenced item changes, your declaration is automatically updated.

```
CREATE OR REPLACE PROCEDURE sp_get_dept_name(v_dept_id IN
dept.id%TYPE,v_dept_name OUT dept.name%TYPE)
AS

BEGIN
   SELECT name INTO v_dept_name FROM dept WHERE id=v_dept_id;

EXCEPTION
   WHEN NO_DATA_FOUND THEN
      DBMS_OUTPUT.put_line('Not Data');

END;
/
```

```
var dept_name VARCHAR2(10)
exec sp_get_dept_name(1,:dept_name)
print dept_name
```

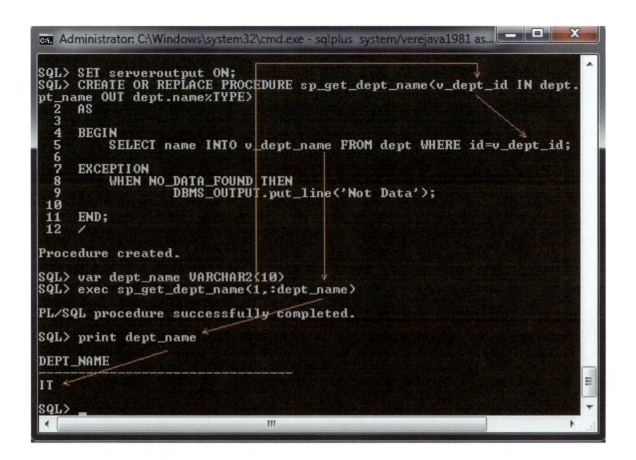

```
SQL> SET serveroutput ON;
SQL> CREATE OR REPLACE PROCEDURE sp_get_dept_name(v_dept_id IN dept.
pt_name OUT dept.name%TYPE)
  2   AS
  3
  4   BEGIN
  5       SELECT name INTO v_dept_name FROM dept WHERE id=v_dept_id;
  6
  7   EXCEPTION
  8       WHEN NO_DATA_FOUND THEN
  9               DBMS_OUTPUT.put_line('Not Data');
 10
 11   END;
 12   /

Procedure created.

SQL> var dept_name VARCHAR2(10)
SQL> exec sp_get_dept_name(1,:dept_name)

PL/SQL procedure successfully completed.

SQL> print dept_name

DEPT_NAME
-----------------------------------

IT

SQL>
```

1. Create a procedure: sp_add_dept Add a new department

```
CREATE OR REPLACE PROCEDURE sp_add_dept(v_dept_id IN dept.id%TYPE,v_name
IN dept.name%TYPE)
AS
BEGIN
    INSERT INTO dept VALUES(v_dept_id,v_name);
END;
/
```

Call the procedure: sp_add_dept

```
EXEC sp_add_dept(4,' Admin');
```

2. Create a procedure: sp_update_dept that modifies dept information

CREATE OR REPLACE PROCEDURE sp_update_dept(v_dept_id IN
dept.id%TYPE,v_name IN dept.name%TYPE)
AS
BEGIN
    UPDATE dept SET name=v_name WHERE id=v_dept_id;
END;
/

Call the procedure: sp_update_dept

EXEC sp_update_dept(4,' Inspect');

2. Create a procedure: sp_delete_dept that delete dept information

```
CREATE OR REPLACE PROCEDURE sp_delete_dept(v_dept_id IN dept.id%TYPE)
AS
BEGIN
     DELETE FROM dept WHERE id=v_dept_id;
END;
/
```

Call the procedure: sp_delete_dept

```
EXEC sp_delete_dept(4)
```

IF Statement

IF-THEN-ELSE statement: is used to execute code when a condition is TRUE, or execute different code if the condition evaluates to FALSE.

Create a procedure: sp_update_salary
Set IT department salary is 1.2 times the original.
Set Finance department salary is 1.5 times the original.

```
CREATE OR REPLACE PROCEDURE sp_update_salary(v_dept_id IN
emp.dept_id%TYPE)
AS

BEGIN
  IF v_dept_id=1 THEN
    UPDATE emp SET salary=salary*1.2 WHERE dept_id=v_dept_id;
  ELSE
    UPDATE emp SET salary=salary*1.5 WHERE dept_id=v_dept_id;
  END IF;

END;
/
```

```
Administrator: C:\Windows\system32\cmd.exe - sqlplus  system/verejava1981 as sy...

SQL> CREATE OR REPLACE PROCEDURE sp_update_salary(v_dept_id IN emp.dep

  2   AS
  3
  4   BEGIN
  5       IF v_dept_id=1 THEN
  6           UPDATE emp SET salary=salary*1.2 WHERE dept_id=v_dept_id;
  7       ELSE
  8           UPDATE emp SET salary=salary*1.5 WHERE dept_id=v_dept_id;
  9       END IF;
 10
 11   END;
 12   /

Procedure created.

SQL>
```

Call the procedure: sp_update_dept

EXEC sp_update_salary (1)

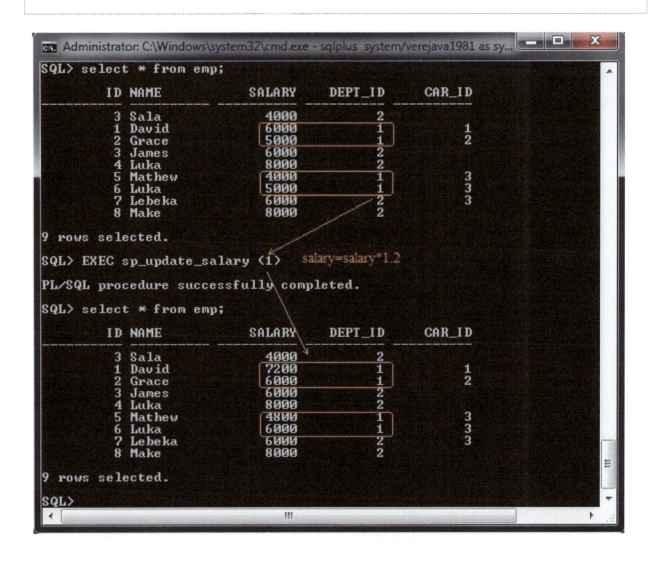

Call the procedure: sp_update_dept

EXEC sp_update_salary (2)

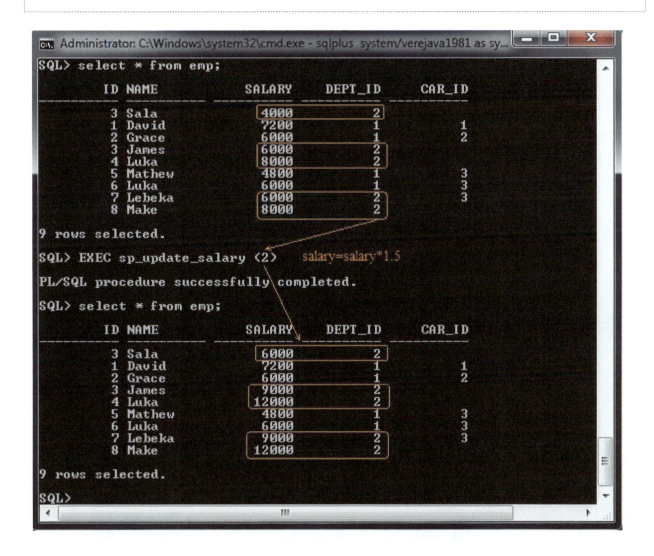

Case Statement

The Oracle/PLSQL CASE statement has the functionality of an IF-THEN-ELSE statement, you can use the CASE statement within a SQL statement.

Create a procedure: sp_update_salary2
Set IT department salary is 2 times the original.
Set Finance department salary is 3 times the original.

```
CREATE OR REPLACE PROCEDURE sp_update_salary2(v_dept_id IN
emp.dept_id%TYPE)

AS

BEGIN
  CASE
    WHEN v_dept_id=1 THEN UPDATE emp SET salary=salary*2 WHERE
dept_id=v_dept_id;
    WHEN v_dept_id=2 THEN UPDATE emp SET salary=salary*3 WHERE
dept_id=v_dept_id;
  END CASE;

END;
/
```

```
Administrator: C:\Windows\system32\cmd.exe - sqlplus  system/verejava1981 as sy...

SQL> CREATE OR REPLACE PROCEDURE sp_update_salary2(v_dept_id IN emp.de
)
  2   AS
  3
  4   BEGIN
  5      CASE
  6          WHEN v_dept_id=1 THEN UPDATE emp SET salary=salary*2 WHER
v_dept_id;
  7          WHEN v_dept_id=2 THEN UPDATE emp SET salary=salary*3 WHER
v_dept_id;
  8      END CASE;
  9
 10   END;
 11   /

Procedure created.

SQL>
```

Call the procedure: sp_update_salary2

EXEC sp_update_salary2 (1)

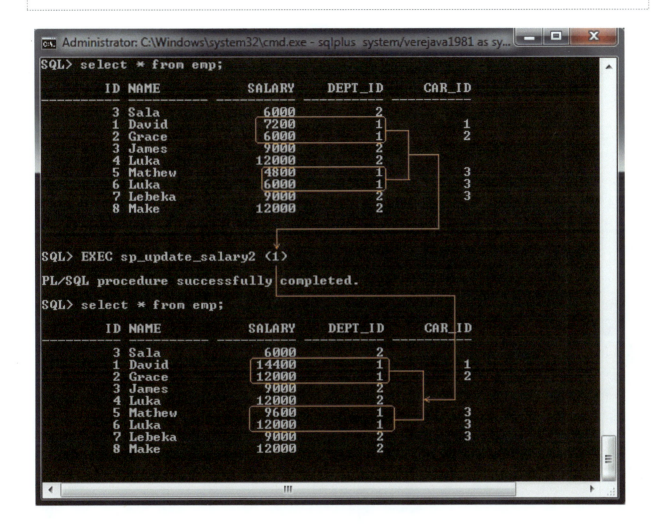

Call the procedure: sp_update_salary2

EXEC sp_update_salary2 (2)

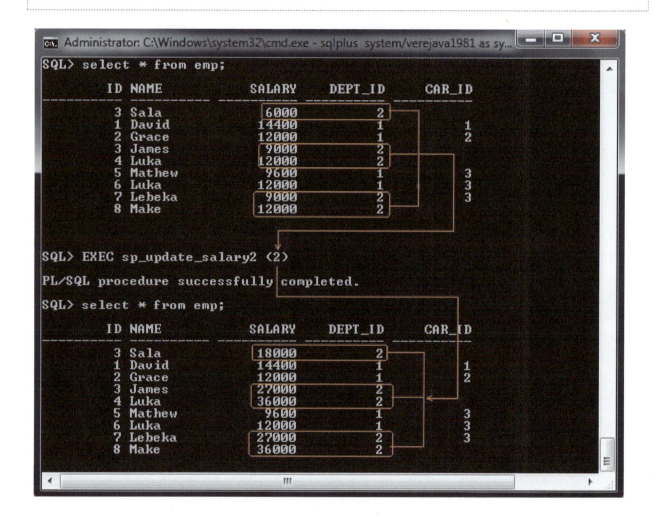

While Loop

WHILE LOOP: when you are not sure how many times you will execute the loop body and the loop body may not execute even once.

Condition:

The condition is tested each pass through the loop. If condition evaluates to TRUE, the loop body is executed. If condition evaluates to FALSE, the loop is terminated.

```
WHILE condition
LOOP
   {...statements...}
END LOOP;
```

Create a procedure: sp_insert_dept Insert more rows into table: dept

```
CREATE OR REPLACE PROCEDURE sp_insert_dept(v_num IN NUMBER)
AS
   i NUMBER(10):=0;
BEGIN
   WHILE i< v_num LOOP
      INSERT INTO dept VALUES(i,'Dept'||i);
      i:=i+1;
   END LOOP;
END;
/
```

```
SQL> CREATE OR REPLACE PROCEDURE sp_insert_dept(v_num IN NUMBER)
  2  AS
  3      i NUMBER(10):=0;
  4  BEGIN
  5      WHILE i< v_num LOOP
  6          INSERT INTO dept VALUES(i,'Dept'||i);
  7          i:=i+1;
  8      END LOOP;
  9  END;
 10  /

Procedure created.

SQL>
```

Delete data from table: emp, dept

DELETE FROM emp;
DELETE FROM dept;

Call the procedure: sp_insert_dept

EXEC sp_insert_dept (3)

```
SQL> DELETE FROM emp;

SQL> DELETE FROM dept;
SQL> CREATE OR REPLACE PROCEDURE sp_insert_dept(v_num IN NUMBER)
  2   AS
  3       i NUMBER(10):=0;
  4   BEGIN
  5       WHILE i< v_num LOOP
  6           INSERT INTO dept VALUES(i,'Dept'||i);
  7           i:=i+1;
  8       END LOOP;
  9   END;
 10   /
SQL> EXEC sp_insert_dept (3)

PL/SQL procedure successfully completed.

SQL> select * from dept;

        ID NAME
---------- ----------
         0 Dept0
         1 Dept1
         2 Dept2

SQL>
```

For Loop

FOR LOOP: allows you to execute code repeatedly for a fixed number of times.

loop_counter: The loop counter variable.
REVERSE: Optional. If specified, the loop counter will count in reverse.
lowest_number: The starting value for loop_counter.
highest_number: The ending value for loop_count

```
FOR loop_counter IN [REVERSE] lowest_number..highest_number
LOOP
   {...statements...}
END LOOP;
```

Insert 3 dept

```
CREATE OR REPLACE PROCEDURE sp_insert_dept2(v_lowest IN NUMBER, v_highest
IN NUMBER)
AS
   i NUMBER(10);
BEGIN
   FOR i IN v_lowest..v_highest LOOP
      INSERT INTO dept VALUES(i,'Dept'||i);
   END LOOP;
END;
/
```

```
SQL> CREATE OR REPLACE PROCEDURE sp_insert_dept2(v_lowest IN NUMBER, v
N NUMBER>
  2  AS
  3       i NUMBER(10);
  4  BEGIN
  5      FOR i IN v_lowest..v_highest LOOP
  6          INSERT INTO dept VALUES(i,'Dept'||i);
  7      END LOOP;
  8  END;
  9  /

Procedure created.

SQL>
```

Call the procedure: sp_insert_dept2

EXEC sp_insert_dept2 (3, 6)

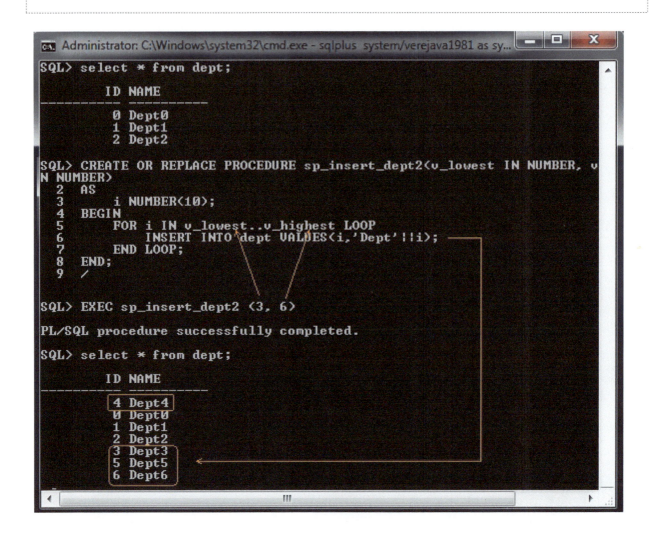

Cursor

Cursor: is a mechanism by which you can assign a name to a SELECT statement and manipulate the information within that SQL statement.

Implicit cursor properties

SQL%ROWCOUNT **:** **number of rows** affected **by SQL**

SQL%FOUND : **Boolean value,** whether there **is data**

SQL%NOTFOUND **:** **Boolean value,** whether there **is no data**

SQL%ISOPEN **:** Implicit cursors **are** always **off,** so always **return FALSE**

Delete data from table: dept, emp

```
DELETE FROM emp;
DELETE FROM dept;
```

Insert data into table: dept

```
INSERT INTO dept(id,name)VALUES(1,'IT');
INSERT INTO dept(id,name)VALUES(2,'Finance');
```

Insert data into table: emp

```
INSERT INTO emp(id,name,salary,dept_id)VALUES(1,'David',6000,1);
INSERT INTO emp(id,name,salary,dept_id)VALUES(2,'James',5000,1);
INSERT INTO emp(id,name,salary,dept_id)VALUES(3,'Grace',6000,2);
INSERT INTO emp(id,name,salary,dept_id)VALUES(4,'Isacc',8000,2);
```

```
SQL> select * from dept;

        ID NAME
---------- ----------
         1 IT
         2 Finance

SQL> select * from emp;

        ID NAME          SALARY    DEPT_ID     CAR_ID
---------- ---------- --------- ---------- ----------
         1 David           6000          1
         2 James           5000          1
         3 Grace           6000          2
         4 Isacc           8000          2
```

Delete emp by dept_id and then display the number of rows deleted

```
CREATE OR REPLACE PROCEDURE sp_delete_emp(v_dept_id IN emp.dept_id%TYPE)
AS
   v_deleted_emp_count NUMBER;
BEGIN
   DELETE FROM emp WHERE dept_id=v_dept_id;
   v_deleted_emp_count:=SQL%ROWCOUNT;
   DBMS_OUTPUT.put_line(v_deleted_emp_count || ' employees were deleted ');
END;
/
```

Call the procedure: sp_delete_emp

```
EXEC sp_delete_emp(2)
```

For Loop Cursor

CURSOR FOR LOOP: when you want to fetch and process every record in a cursor. The CURSOR FOR LOOP will terminate when all of the records in the cursor have been fetched.

Use cursor for loop to display the names of all departments

```
DECLARE
   CURSOR c_dept IS SELECT * FROM dept;
   c_row c_dept%ROWTYPE;
BEGIN
   FOR c_row in c_dept LOOP
      DBMS_OUTPUT.put_line('Dept Name : ' || c_row.name);
   END LOOP;
END;
/
```

Fetch Cursor

The purpose of using a cursor, in most cases, is to retrieve the rows from your cursor so that some type of operation can be performed on the data. After declaring and opening your cursor, the next step is to use the FETCH statement to fetch rows from your cursor.

Print the names and salaries of all emp
   SQL%FOUND : Boolean value, whether there **is data**
   SQL%NOTFOUND : **Boolean value,** whether there **is no data**

```
DECLARE
   CURSOR c_emp IS SELECT name,salary FROM emp;
   c_row c_emp%ROWTYPE;
BEGIN
   OPEN c_emp;
   FETCH c_emp INTO c_row;
   WHILE c_emp%FOUND LOOP
      DBMS_OUTPUT.put_line(c_row.name ||',' || c_row.salary);
      FETCH c_emp INTO c_row;
   END LOOP;
   CLOSE c_emp;
END;
/
```

Trigger

trigger: is a named PL/SQL block stored in the Oracle Database and executed automatically when a triggering event takes place. The event can be any of the following: A data manipulation language (DML) statement executed against a table e.g., INSERT , UPDATE , or DELETE .

:NEW The value of the column after the operation is completed
:OLD The value of the previous column before the operation is completed

	INSERT	UPDATE	DELETE
:OLD	NULL	Actual value	Actual value
:NEW	Actual value	Actual value	NULL

Trigger predicate

INSERTING returns TRUE if the INSERT statement is triggered, otherwise FALSE
UPDATING returns TRUE if the UPDATE statement is triggered, otherwise FALSE
DELETING returns TRUE if a DELETE statement is triggered, otherwise FALSE

Create a table: emp_log that save log of table: emp

```
CREATE TABLE emp_log
(
  id NUMBER(10),
  name VARCHAR2(10),
  salary NUMBER(10),
  dept_id NUMBER(10),
  car_id NUMBER(10),
  type VARCHAR2(10),
  current_user VARCHAR2(20)
);
```

Create a trigger: tr_emp_log **When the table emp is deleted, when the previous record is modified, the affected records are backup into the table:** emp_log.

Create a Trigger : tr_emp_log

```sql
CREATE OR REPLACE TRIGGER tr_emp_log
   BEFORE DELETE OR  UPDATE
   ON emp
   FOR EACH ROW
BEGIN

   IF DELETING THEN
     INSERT INTO
emp_log(current_user,id,name,salary,dept_id,type)VALUES(SYS_CONTEXT('USERENV','
CURRENT_USER'),:OLD.id,:OLD.name,:OLD.salary,:OLD.dept_id,'delete');
   END IF;
   IF UPDATING THEN
     INSERT INTO
emp_log(current_user,id,name,salary,dept_id,type)VALUES(SYS_CONTEXT('USERENV','
CURRENT_USER'),:OLD.id,:OLD.name,:OLD.salary,:OLD.dept_id,'update');
   END IF;
END;
/
```

Update table: emp, the trigger: tr_emp_log will call automatically
UPDATING insert log of data to table: emp_log

UPDATE emp SET salary=10000 WHERE name='David';
SELECT * FROM emp_log;

Delete data from table: emp, the trigger: tr_emp_log will call automatically
DELETING insert log of data to table: emp_log

DELETE FROM emp WHERE name='David';
SELECT * FROM emp_log;

Thanks for learning

https://www.amazon.com/dp/B08HTXMXVY

https://www.amazon.com/dp/B08BWT6RCT

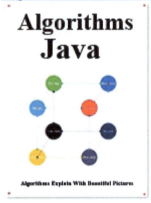

http://en.verejava.com/

If you enjoyed this book and found some benefit in reading this, I'd like to hear from you and hope that you could take some time to post a review on Amazon. Your feedback and support will help us to greatly improve in future and make this book even better.

You can follow this link now.

http://www.amazon.com/review/create-review?&asin=1094789100

Different country reviews only need to modify the amazon domain name in the link:
www.amazon.co.uk
www.amazon.de
www.amazon.fr
www.amazon.es
www.amazon.it
www.amazon.ca
www.amazon.nl
www.amazon.in
www.amazon.co.jp
www.amazon.com.br
www.amazon.com.mx
www.amazon.com.au

I wish you all the best in your future success!

www.ingramcontent.com/pod-product-compliance
Lightning Source LLC
Chambersburg PA
CBHW041427050326
40689CB00003B/689